Devon A-Z

Paul White

Bossiney Books

Some other Bossiney titles you might find interesting

Book lover's Devon
Devon's railway heritage
Devon castles
Devon's history
Devon smugglers: the truth behind the fiction
Sir Francis Drake – Devon's flawed hero
Tales from Devon folklore
Ten Town Trails: South Devon

Shortish Guides
Dartmouth
Exeter
Plymouth
South Hams

First published 2016
by Bossiney Books Ltd, 33 Queens Drive, Ilkley, LS29 9QW
www.bossineybooks.com
© 2016 Paul White   All rights reserved
ISBN 978-1-906474-53-9

Printed in Great Britain by R Booth Ltd, Penryn, Cornwall

Aemilius

Aemilius, son of Saenius, *civis Dumnonius* (citizen of Dumnonia, or Devon), is the first British sailor whose name is known to us. A funerary inscription to him was found at Cologne, where he had served in the Roman fleet on the Rhine.

Arsenic and William Morris

William Morris (1834-1896) is famous for his role in the Arts and Crafts movement, but also for his Marxist Socialism, though that was always much stronger in theory than in his practice as an employer.

His father and uncles were major investors at the start of Devon Great Consolidated Copper Mining Co., later known as Devon Great Consols, which from 1844 mined land just east of the Tamar owned by the Duke of Bedford. His father held 272 out of 1024 shares when the firm started.

It was a risky venture which became an astonishing success, one of the most profitable mineral mines in the world. William Morris was given shares when he came of age, and these made him a wealthy man in his own right, enabling him to follow his artistic interests and establish his own decorative arts company, which among other things made wallpapers to Morris's famous designs.

These wallpapers used a green pigment made from arsenic, which is of course highly poisonous. Some doctors believed that when these wallpapers were used on damp walls, and mould developed, they released a gas and arsenic poisoning resulted. Morris would have none of it, saying 'My belief about it all is that the doctors find their patients ailing, don't know what's the matter with them, and in despair put it down to the wall papers.' There was no reliable evidence either way, but this was a pretty cavalier approach to a serious question – and of course a highly convenient one.

The question of hypocrisy becomes more serious when it is realised that from 1870 onwards, when its copper resources declined, Devon Great Consols was producing half the British output of arsenic. William Morris was a director from 1871 to 1875, when he sold his shares in order to invest more in his own business. He seems to have preferred not to know too much about the working conditions in the mine, where the arsenic certainly did pose a threat to the workers' health.

Sabine Baring-Gould

The Reverend Sabine Baring-Gould (1834-1924) was a most remarkable man. For the last 43 years of his life he was both squire and parson ('squarson') of Lewtrenchard, between Okehampton and Launceston. Much of his childhood had been spent travelling in Europe with his parents, and by the age of fifteen he spoke five languages fluently: this gave him a broad cultural background unusual in an English clergyman and at the same time he was blessed with phenomenal energy.

He became known as a great collector of folk-songs (preceding and then collaborating with Cecil Sharp) and as a writer of stirring hymns – 'Onward Christian soldiers' and 'Through the night of doubt and sorrow' are both his. He was a key player in the study and preservation of the prehistoric remains on Dartmoor. In between times he was architect and site supervisor for building his own house, supported a huge extended family, and fathered fifteen children – though there is a story that on one occasion he asked a little girl, 'Whose child are you, my dear?' only to be answered 'Yours, Daddy.'

He was also a prolific writer with well over a hundred titles to his credit on everything from theology to *How to save fuel* and *A History of Sarawak under its Two White Rajahs*. His prose, like his personality, is robust and dynamic and his writing about Devon and Cornwall was immensely popular in his day.

A great deal of the information in his books was taken from his extraordinarily voluminous memory, rather than checking back with the original sources. His unquenchable self-confidence in his own abilities and judgement in this respect, as in everything he undertook, mean he can sometimes be faulted in matters of detail.

Although forthright in his opinions and having marked prejudices (especially against Methodists) he was no snob. During his first curacy at Horbury near Wakefield he had married Grace Taylor, daughter of a mill-hand, and it is said to have been a very happy marriage. (She must have been a very tolerant woman!) He also seems to have got on well with the old men of Dartmoor from whom, by the pub firesides, he collected the words and tunes of their traditional music, though whether he understood them or the majority of his parishioners quite as well as he imagined, is perhaps to be doubted.

Cobley, Uncle Tom (and sundry others)

The Tom Cobley who went to Widecombe Fair (see page 11) may have been a real person, who lived to the north of the moor. There was a family near Spreyton in which the name Thomas was favoured, and there are several records of baptisms, marriages and burials which might be 'Uncle Tom Cobley'. A tax record of 1798 shows a Thomas Cobley Jnr renting a property to another Thomas Cobley, at an annual rent of £2. 0s. 4d.

Local historians incline to think that the folk song refers to a Thomas Cobley who died in 1794, having lived at Butsford Barton, Colebrooke, and whose will survives.

He reputedly never married, but was the recipient of rather a large number of paternity orders from the parish. Having very distinctive red hair, he refused to accept any responsibility to maintain babies who did not share this trait. If this *is* the man in the song, he may well have been 'Uncle' to quite a few nephews and nieces.

Crying the neck

This was a West Country harvest custom until the nineteenth century, and apparently it has been revived in Cornwall. Mrs Bray, wife of the vicar of Tavistock, provided a fine description of the custom in 1836 – though like many of her generation she was obsessed with Druidism.

> One evening about the end of harvest I was riding out on my pony, attended by my servant who was born and bred a Devonian. We were passing near a field on the borders of Dartmoor, where the reapers were assembled. In a moment the pony started nearly from one side of the way to the other, so sudden came a shout from the field, which gave him this alarm. On my stopping to ask my servant what all the noise was about, he seemed surprised by the question, and said, 'It was only the people making their games, as they always did, to the spirit of the harvest.' I felt certain here was to be observed some curious vestige of an ancient superstition, and I soon gained all the information I could wish to obtain upon the subject.
>
> When the reaping is finished, toward evening the labourers select some of the best ears of corn from the sheaves; these they tie together and it is called the nack. Sometimes, as it was when I witnessed the custom, this nack is decorated with flowers, twisted in with reed, which gives it a gay and fantastic appearance. The reapers then proceed to a high place, to 'holla the nack'. The man who bears this offering stands in the midst and elevates it whilst all the other labourers form themselves into a circle about him. Each holds aloft his hook and in a

moment they all shout, as loud as they possibly can, these words, which I spell as I heard them pronounced:

'Arnack, arnack, arnack, wehaven, wehaven, wehaven.'

This is repeated three separate times, and the firkin is handed round between each shout by way of libation. When the weather is fine, different parties of reapers, each stationed on some height, may be heard from miles round, as it were in answer to each other.

The evening I witnessed the ceremony, many women and children, some carrying boughs and others having flowers in their caps or in their hands or in their bonnets, were seen, some dancing, others singing, whilst the men practised the rights in a ring. Can we for a moment doubt that this custom is a vestige of Druidism?

Sarah Hewitt, in *Nummits and Crummits* (1900) tells us that after the ceremony in the field

> … the cider-firkin was passed around from mouth to mouth. Then a start was made for the farmer's kitchen, where a substantial amount of pork, beef, vegetables, figgy-pudden, cream, junkets, and gallons of cider awaited the hungry reapers, as well as the farmer's wife and his older children. When justice had been done to the food, long churchwarden pipes were produced, and more cider provoked merriment and indescribable tumult. Some recounted their experiences in winter, in snowstorms or floods, or their meetings with the Devil on lonely hills, or wanderings over swampy meadows in the footsteps of Jack-o'Lantern. Others sang the old songs, or songs they had themselves composed, and not until daylight streamed in did they seek their beds.

The neck was hung up over the kitchen table, and last year's neck was given to the best beast in the cow-shed.

Benjamin Donn – map-maker

Benjamin Donn was baptised at Bideford on 22 June 1729. He was the youngest child of George Donn, who was the Parish Clerk and ran the local school, where his speciality was practical maths and science – useful to the future merchants of Bideford – and navigation which was invaluable to its sailors.

Benjamin became a regular contributor to the *Mathematical Repository* and to the *Gentleman's Magazine*, and he subsequently published books about maths, accountancy and navigation.

The body which later became the Royal Society of Arts offered in 1759 a prize for producing the first accurately surveyed map of a county, and Benjamin won this prize with his one-inch-to-the-mile map of Devon, published in 1765. The prize was £100, and the survey work took him 5 years costing him £2000, but the backing of the Society helped him raise the remaining funds, mainly by subscriptions. The map was engraved by the leading London mapmaker of the day, and is extremely elegant: a facsimile was published in book form in 1965.

In 1768 Donn was elected Librarian of the Bristol Library, where he produced a map of the area in 1769, and also started an academy there. Later he settled near Taunton, and he died in 1798.

The Earl of Rone

The 'Hunting of the Earl of Rone' is an ancient custom celebrated at Combe Martin at the Spring Bank Holiday, though it was formerly celebrated on Ascension Day, which falls on the Thursday forty days after Easter. The custom was suppressed in 1837 because of licentiousness and drunken behaviour. It was revived in 1974.

A description of the pre-Victorian custom said:

> A procession was formed of mummers, one representing the Earl wearing a grotesque mask, a smock-frock and twelve sea-biscuits strung around his neck; a hobby-horse masked and armed with a 'mapper' – an instrument shaped like a horse's mouth with teeth, and able to be snapped open and shut; a fool, masked; a donkey, also with a necklace of biscuits; and a troop of grenadiers armed with guns. On Ascension Day the grenadiers marched to Lady's Wood, near the village, and found the Earl of Rone hidden in the brushwood. They fired a volley, set him on the donkey with his face to the tail, and thus took him through the village to the sea, joined by the hobby-horse and the fool. At certain points the grenadiers fired and the Earl fell, mortally wounded. The spectators had to contribute to the drinks fund; if they did not, the hobby-horse laid hold of them with his teeth.

Some say this is the relic of a pagan custom associated with May Day, and the Hobby-Horse has similarities with those at Padstow and Minehead. Others believe it has a historical basis, with the 'Earl of Rone' being Hugh O'Neill, Earl of Tyrone who, along with the Earl of Tyrconnell, The Maguire and 90 followers, fled from Donegal. They reached Normandy on 4 October 1607, but an old Devonian tradition (with no historical evidence for or against) said they landed, or were ship-wrecked, in Rapparee Cove, Ilfracombe, and were subsequently picked up living in the woods surviving on sea biscuits. Probably the Hunting is a joyous mish-mash of many ideas, and certainly today no-one takes the history seriously.

The revived custom has its own website, which has much more information both on the modern festivities and their history.

Fairs and mares

There were of course many traditional fairs in Devon, but two in particular stand out, not least because each has a folk song associated with it – Widecombe Fair and Tavistock Goosey Fair.

Goosey Fair has been held on the second Wednesday of October since 1823, being originally a Michaelmas fair. The name probably originates from the sale of geese to be fattened up for Christmas dinner, in the days before turkeys became customary. It attracts large numbers of market stalls, and a funfair makes it a major event in Tavistock's calendar.

'Tavvystock Goozey Vair' is a folk-song first published in 1912 as the work of Charles John Trythall (1864-1936), an accountancy clerk with the GWR, who was born in Plymouth but spent most of his career in London. Some people imagine Trythall collected a traditional song, but it is more likely he composed it himself: those Paddington offices must have made him nostalgic for Devon.

> Us went to see the 'orses
> And the 'effers and the yews.
> Us went on all them roundabouts
> And into all the shows,
> And then it started raining
> And blowing in our face,
> So off us goes down to the Rose
> To 'ave a dish of tay.
>
> And then us had a sing song
> And the folks kept dropping in,
> And what with one an' t'other,
> Well, us had a drop of gin,
> And what with one an' t'other,
> Us didn't seem to care

> Whether us was to Bellever Tor
> Or Tavistock Goosey Fair.
>
>> *And it's oh, and where be a-going,*
>> *And what be a-doing of there.*
>> *Heave down your prong and stamp along,*
>> *To Tavistock Goosey Fair.*
>
> 'Twere raining streams and dark as pitch
> When us trotted 'ome that night,
> An' when us got past Merrivale Bridge,
> Our mare, 'er took a fright.
> Says I to Bill, 'Be careful,
> You'll 'ave us in them drains.'
> Says 'e to me, 'Cor bugger, why,
> 'Aven't *you* got the reins?'

Widecombe Fair is of unknown origin, and in the nineteenth century seems to have been a cattle fair, but today it has multiple attractions, and draws large crowds of visitors. The song was first recorded by Sabine Baring-Gould, an early collector of folk songs, and published in 1890. The list of people who travelled to the fair (Uncle Tom Cobley and all – see page 5) just might be a list of real people, who travelled from Spreyton in 1802, and the song may be an account of a real event, so we should perhaps mourn Tom Pearce's old mare, and maybe watch out for her ghost:

> When the wind whistles cold on the moor of the night,
> All along, down along, out along leas,
> Tom Pearce's old mare doth appear ghastly white,
> With Bill Brewer, Jan Stewer, Peter Gurney,
> Peter Davy, Dan'l Whiddon, Harry Hawke,
> Old Uncle Tom Cobley and all,
> Old Uncle Tom Cobley and all.

Fawlty Towers

The two series, each of six episodes, are regarded as one of the best TV sitcoms of all time. First broadcast in 1975, its inspiration came when the *Monty Python* team including John Cleese were filming on location in Torquay, and stayed at the Gleneagles Hotel on

Asheldon Road, not far from Kent's Cavern.

At the time (1971) it was owned by Donald Sinclair, whose bizarre behaviour (as perceived by John Cleese) was the model for Basil Fawlty – a mixture of rudeness, snobbery, and a belief that he could run a superb hotel if only the guests didn't keep getting in the way. As in the series, Sinclair's wife Beatrice was actually in control of the business, which she had herself started: Donald Sinclair only became involved when he retired from the Navy.

At the time of writing, the hotel was still open. The council planners rejected proposals, in 2003 and 2014, to turn the site into a block of flats. No part of the TV series was shot in Devon.

Green Man

No fewer than 87 of Devon's churches, including Exeter Cathedral which is said to have more than 30 examples, contain carvings representing 'the Green Man'. These are male heads usually sprouting branches or leaves from the mouths, noses and even tear ducts, but sometimes the faces themselves are constructed out of leaves. There is no single pattern, and each craftsman seems to have let his imagination free. The name 'Green Man' was only invented in 1939.

Originally it seems to have been a motif from ancient Rome, and it is found across the whole of Europe, almost exclusively in churches – but quite why is a mystery. Some people assume it represents a pagan fertility spirit, in which case it is either the work of subversive carvers (unlikely) or it is a representation of evil. Some say it is a symbol of mortality, or of resurrection. It could well be associated with May Day and the figure of Jack-in-the-Green who dances around dressed as a tree.

But the truth is that nobody knows, and there seems to be no reference to the Green Man carvings in medieval writings – though of course one of the finest medieval poems is *Sir Gawain and the Green Knight*.

Grenville and 'The Revenge'

Anyone born before 1945 will probably remember from primary school, 'At Flores in the Azores Sir Richard Grenville lay,' the first line of Tennyson's ballad 'The Revenge'. It was imperial propaganda. But was Sir Richard really a hero? A contemporary described him as 'a man of intolerable pride and insatiable ambition.'

The Grenvilles were lords of the manor of Bideford, and of Stowe and Kilkhampton just across the border in Cornwall. Richard's father was master of the *Mary Rose* and drowned when it capsized. Richard (1542-1591) inherited at the age of nine.

He spent some time at the Inns of Court, which were the normal finishing school for gentlemen. In 1562 he killed a man in a street brawl – gangs of sword-toting young bloods were a feature of London life – but since the dead man was only a yeoman and Grenville was an aristocrat, he was soon pardoned. His Devon possessions were extensive, including Buckland Abbey, which he rebuilt in its present form, and the whole town of Bideford which he set about developing with a new quay and a town charter, giving up some of his manorial privileges but creating a bustling and profitable port.

He was financially interested in various privateering ventures, as well as a proposal for a voyage to discover the supposed North-West Passage and explore the Pacific – but this was probably just an excuse for piracy. The Queen vetoed it.

In the event it was Francis Drake (seen by Grenville as a low-born upstart) who made his fame and fortune from a round-the-world voyage, and on his return eclipsed Grenville as the leading man in the Plymouth area. Seething quietly, Grenville sold Buckland Abbey, only to find that Drake immediately snapped it up. Grenville's general policy was to sell his remoter estates, and consolidate around Bideford and Kilkhampton.

In 1585 he made what seems to have been his first major voyage, to establish the Roanoke colony in north Carolina. Grenville took some lucrative prizes on his way back. Returning the following year with supplies, he found the base deserted. That man Drake had rescued the survivors a few weeks previously. This time on the way back Grenville sacked towns in the Azores.

By now war with Spain was becoming serious and Grenville was instructed to stay in England and lend his ships to Drake as part of the defence against the Armada. Drake later took *The Revenge* for his attack on Lisbon. This expedition was disastrous: Drake was now sidelined (one can imagine Grenville's glee) and a new policy instituted. An English fleet would hover in the Atlantic to intercept the Spanish treasure fleets.

Consequently, in 1591 Sir Richard Grenville, under the command of Lord Thomas Howard, lay indeed at Flores in the Azores refitting his ship. The Spanish, however, knew what the English were up to and sent a vastly larger fleet (tradition says 53 ships) to pounce on them.

Admiral Howard was warned, and he ordered a tactical withdrawal. All the other English ships got away, but Grenville seems to have deliberately delayed, then chose to sail into the middle of the Spanish fleet, where a galleon three times the tonnage of *The Revenge* grappled her and tried to board. An epic battle followed.

The fight continued through the night and by dawn *The Revenge* was a dismasted wreck surrounded by Spanish ships, two of which later sank. Honourable terms were offered, but Grenville (knowing himself fatally wounded) wanted to blow up or sink his ship. He was prevented by the officers. He was given the best care possible by the Spanish, who recorded his last words, which consisted of pride in his own achievement and scorn for the men who had chosen not to die – but the scorn was omitted from the English translation when it was circulated.

Tennyson's poem gave a rose-coloured view of the final action. Modern interpretations suggest that Sir Richard had deliberately disobeyed an order and sacrificed his men, the objectives of Lord Howard's mission, and one of England's best ships, all for personal glory or in a fit of battle madness.

The Hound of the Baskervilles

Possibly the second best known novel set in Devon (second to *Sense and Sensibility*), the *Hound* has for better or worse provided the reading public with a very misleading and Romantic view of Dartmoor: '…this most God-forsaken corner of the world. The longer one stays here the more does the spirit of the moor sink into one's soul, its vastness and all its grim charm.'

It is of course, unlike the other Sherlock Holmes stories, a late gothic novel, and Conan Doyle exaggerates the unusual features of the moor, with Dr Watson apparently losing all sense of objective reality in his response to these unfamiliar surroundings. This is in contrast to Holmes himself, who seems able to negotiate the moor at night with as few problems as if he'd been using a Bossiney Walks Book and a pocket torch.

Conan Doyle's own knowledge of Dartmoor was rather limited. In 1882 he spent a few weeks in Plymouth, hoping to form a joint medical practice with Dr George Budd, a friend from his student days. But the two men's personalities clashed and Conan Doyle soon left to pursue his medical career elsewhere. He did, however, return to Devon that same autumn for a photographic holiday, walking from Plymouth to Tavistock until the expedition was terminated by rain, but not before he had succumbed to Dartmoor's 'grim charm'.

In 1900 he formed a friendship with the journalist Bertram Fletcher Robinson of Ipplepen, and they decided to collaborate on a Dartmoor book, staying briefly at the Duchy Hotel in Princetown. How much influence Robinson had on the book is unknown – probably very little since it became a Sherlock Holmes story, but he may have contributed knowledge of Devon folklore, especially of hell-hounds, including the phantom pack which haunted the tomb of Squire Richard Cabell who died in 1677, a tomb which is still there near the ruined old church at Buckfastleigh, and which canophobes should visit only with extreme caution…

Industrial Devon

This may sound like a contradiction in terms. Most visitors remain unaware even of what remains of Devon's industries, which the county tends to hide, especially the extractive industries which so spoil the landscape.

In historical terms, we tend to think of agriculture and fishing as being typical, but this was far from the case. Devon in 1700 – before 'industry' meant factories – was regarded as an industrial county. Daniel Defoe, in *A Tour through Great Britain* (1724) wrote: 'Devonshire … is so full of great towns, and those towns so full of people, and those people so universally employed in trade and manufactures, that not only it cannot be equalled in England, but perhaps not in Europe.'

Perhaps most surprising was the cloth trade. Devon as a base for woollen manufacture had shared several characteristics with the Pennines – upland areas unsuitable for much other than grazing sheep, Cistercian monasteries keen to exploit the wastelands, rivers strong enough to power numerous fulling mills (known in Devon as tucking mills) and soft water with which to treat the wool.

The cloth trade can be traced back to the 12th century, with Exeter ranked seventh in England in 1202. It had taken off in a big way by the 15th century. Much of the cloth was exported, especially from Exeter, which became the wealthiest wool market in the country, until overtaken by Leeds around 1700.

There were many types of cloth, dependent on the nature of the wool (wool from sheep on the western side of Dartmoor produced coarser cloth) and on the methods of manufacture and especially finishing. High quality 'kerseys' were Devon's main output in the middle ages, 'serges' (also known as 'perpetuanos' because they were long-lasting) after 1600. Fashions changed over the years, and some Devon towns lost out through failure to adapt, for example Totnes, which became very rich in the Tudor period but continued making the same kind of 'narrow-pin-whites' and suffered for it. Some tried to change: Tiverton sent spies to Norwich, which had invented a new method, and they only narrowly escaped with their lives. In 1752 a Tiverton firm started making Norwich 'stuffs', but the copy-cat enterprise soon failed.

Devon's textile industry would ultimately lose out to Yorkshire, where coal was available for the new steam-powered mills, and to cheap cotton goods. Apart from an outpost at Buckfastleigh, the industry rapidly collapsed, and the effects were all the more disastrous to the local economy because another major cottage industry, lace-making, went into decline at the same time.

Mining was also a significant industry at certain periods: Devon was usually overshadowed by Cornwall, but from about 1160-1210 fresh discoveries of tin made Devon Europe's largest producer, and in the nineteenth century Devon Great Consols in the Tamar valley was a huge producer of copper. Dartmoor has numerous remains of tin extraction, mostly from the Tudor and Victorian periods. Mining has not ceased: a new tungsten mine opened at Hemerdon near Plymouth in 2015.

Because of its very diverse geology, Devon has always been a source of building stone, from the characteristic stone of the Beer area to Dartmoor granite. A wide area of ball clay north of Newton Abbot has been supplying the pottery industry for centuries, and China clay from south Dartmoor goes to make glossy paper – and perhaps some porcelain, which was its earliest use.

Paper-making too was a significant industry in the days when paper was made mainly from rags, and benefitted from the same rivers and water quality as woollen manufacture, but Devon was ill placed to import Scandinavian timber once that became the favoured raw material. At one time there were 25 paper mills, now there appears to be just one.

The Joannites

This was the name given to the followers of Joanna Southcott, 'the Exeter prophetess'.

She was the daughter of a small farmer, born in 1750 at Taleford north of Ottery St Mary, was brought up in Gittisham, and spent many years in Exeter, working for an upholsterer. She was always very religious, and worshipped twice every Sunday in Exeter Cathedral, and additionally at Methodist meetings. At the age of 42 she had 'ten days experience of the powers of darkness' (perhaps we might call it a breakdown) then began scribbling prophecies in verse. Some of these, for example about bad harvests, appeared to come true, though the cynic may argue that their totally illegible handwriting and impenetrable expression of nonsense were in the best tradition of Merlin and Mother Shipton – prophecies which 'cannot be understood until their fulfilment'.

In 1802 she published *The Strange Effects of Faith*, and gradually some clergy came to take her seriously. It was revealed to her that she was the woman predicted in the *Book of Revelations*, 12:1-6 – 'a woman clothed with the sun, and the moon under her feet, and upon her head a crown of twelve stars'.

In the same year she moved to London, and began the lucrative business of selling certificates proving that a believer was one of the 144,000 faithful who were guaranteed a place in heaven. A chapel was opened for her followers in Southwark in 1805. In 1813, at the age of 63, she declared herself to be a virgin pregnant with Shiloh, 'the second Christ'.

Hundreds of pounds were donated for cribs and infant paraphernalia. No child was born: she died in December 1814, failed to rise again as she had prophesied, and was buried in St John's Wood.

A codicil to her will made provision for the 'monies, various articles of plate and other things intended for the male child which I announced would be born' to be returned to the donors if no child was born. Whilst she certainly profited from her prophecies, she was a very moral person – and there is no doubt she believed in her own divine mission.

Her numerous followers (perhaps 100,000 of them) were known as the Joannites, though some now call them the Southcottians. Astonishingly, though their numbers declined, some were still active in the 20th century, and the last member of a Bedford group, the Panacea Society, died in 2012.

After her death an article in *The Edinburgh Review* concluded:

> Upon the whole, the mission of Joanna Southcott is an extremely curious article in the history of human credulity. But while we laugh at the simplicity of her disciples, we may all of us do well to look homeward, and to consider whether our own belief is not on various occasions determined by our feelings, more than by evidence – whether we are not sometimes duped by respected names or bold pretenders – and sometimes by our own fancies, fears or wishes.

Rudyard Kipling (1865-1936)

Kipling was a much-travelled man, who in 1896 was living in America. A now-forgotten argument between the USA and Britain (concerning a dispute between Britain and Venezuela about British Guiana) decided him to return to Britain, and he settled at Rock House in Torquay. It was there that he wrote *Stalky and Co.*, about his own educational experiences at the United Services College in Westward Ho!

Unfortunately the Kiplings found a problem with their house. It might have been the drains, but in *The Mark of the Beast* he wrote:

> ... a gathering blackness of mind and sorrow of the heart, that each put down to the new, soft climate, and, without telling the other, fought against for long weeks. It was the Feng-shui – the Spirit of the house itself – that darkened the sunshine and fell upon us every time we entered, checking the very words on our lips... We paid forfeit and left.

This experience inspired a short story, 'The House Surgeon', a tale of the paranormal which includes the phrase:

> 'Then I shall be chained to the rock all my life' she went on. 'Only don't tell papa.'

For 'the rock' read 'Rock House'? Moreover, Kipling, supposedly such an exemplary Victorian, was less than enamoured of Torquay:

> Torquay is such a place as I do desire to upset it by dancing through it with nothing on but my spectacles. Villas, clipped hedges and shaven lawns, fat old ladies with respirators and obese landaus.

Lydford Law

> I oft have heard of Lydford Law,
> How in the morn they hang and draw
> And sit in judgement after.
> At first I wondered at it much;
> But now I find their reason such,
> That it deserves no laughter.
>
> They have a castle on a hill;
> I took it for an old windmill,
> The vanes blown off by weather.
> Than lie therein on night, 'tis guessed,

'Tis better to be ston'd or press'd,
Or hang'd, now choose you whether.

Ten men less room within this cave
Than five mice in a lanthorn have;
The keepers they are sly ones:
If any could devise by art
To get it up upon a cart,
'Twere fit to carry lions.

When I beheld it, Lord! thought I,
What justice and what clemency
Hath Lydford, when I spy all!
They know none there would gladly stay,
But rather hang out of the way,
Than tarry for his trial.

These verses published in 1644 were by the Tavistock poet William Browne, whose 'Lydford Journey' is a satire against the poverty and perhaps the pretensions of the neighbouring 'town' of Lydford.

Lydford, before the Norman conquest, had been on a par with Exeter, but had greatly declined. Nevertheless, the parish of Lydford included the whole of Dartmoor (it was the largest parish in England until divided in 1987) and the castle served as the place of judgement and also as the prison for both Forest Law, which applied to poachers, and Stannary Law which governed the tin industry.

Anyone found guilty of breaking these laws (and the burden of proof was not high) could be imprisoned in Lydford Castle to await sentencing. Unfortunately the Court responsible for sentencing met only once every three years. The gaolers had no wish to waste the king's resources on keeping the prisoners fed, so if a death sentence was likely (as it often was under Forest Law) they executed the prisoners immediately. Perhaps it was, as Browne's satire suggests, the most merciful course of action.

'Lydford Law' became synonymous with injustice.

Mixed bathing

This was a big issue in Victorian Britain. Back in the eighteenth century wealthy visitors went to the seaside for medicinal purposes, to drink sea water [!] and be 'dipped' either in the sea or in baths of sea-water, rather than for the pleasure of swimming. Few of them came to Devon. Meanwhile, as early as 1750 a visitor described Exmouth as 'a place to which the people of Exeter much resort for diversion and bathing in the sea'. These were ordinary people, not the wealthy, and they arrived on Saturday afternoons.

By 1779 rich visitors had started coming to Exmouth and were shocked by 'shoals of Exeter damsels, whose insufferable undress and ill breeding justly exposes them to the contempt and derision of strangers'. There was only mixed bathing at this period, and it is likely that the men and some at least of the women bathed naked.

Even when bathing machines were introduced, there was no segregation for fashionable bathers. But in 1800 *The Observer* objected to 'the indecency of numerous naked men bathing in the sea close to the ladies' bathing machines'.

Pressure mounted during the century, as prudery increased, but there had also been a change in the nature of fashionable sea bathing. No longer was it an ordeal briefly undertaken for the sake of one's health: now it was fun, and people spent longer at the beach – which made beaches more crowded. And it seems to be a fact that, for most of the Victorian period, people delighted in the seaside as a place where the stifling decorum of their times could be totally ignored.

Men were still bathing naked, and ladies' bathing garments were incompatible with swimming. *The Observer*, still preoccupied with the subject, in 1856 noted:

> Females do not venture beyond the surf and lay themselves

on their backs, waiting for the coming waves... The waves come and carry their dresses up to their neck, so that as far as decency is concerned they might as well be without any dresses at all... and all this takes place in the presence of thousands of spectators...

A growing number of working people used cheap-day-return rail tickets to have a quick dip: they could not afford bathing machines and, at Dawlish for example, when the cheap train arrived, men and women alike rushed to the beach to strip off and run into the sea. Those wealthy visitors staying in Dawlish were scandalised – or were they?

Whilst the pressure for local legislation to forbid nude bathing and to enforce segregation had some effect, commercial pressure was ambivalent and bye-laws were poorly enforced. True, some visitors were appalled and did not return, but resorts where naked bathing took place were usually crowded, especially at high tide. Ladies 'outraged decorum by viewing from the pier and the beach, through opera glasses, the antics of nude gentlemen.'

Nevertheless by the end of the century things had changed at some resorts, especially those such as Torquay which had high social pretensions. (Agatha Christie's *Autobiography* has an amusing section about the horrors of bathing machines in the Ladies' Bathing Cove, where the Torquay Yacht Club had its premises on the cliff above, and it was the gentlemen who had the opera glasses.) In the posh resorts, central beaches were carefully segregated – but the outer beaches were often open to all.

By the 1890s the press had changed their tune: there was pressure to *end* segregation, so that families could be together, and men could teach their womenfolk to swim. Paignton led the way in 1896, but insisted on neck-to-knee costumes for both sexes in the mixed bathing area. Bathing machines went swiftly out of use, but bathing tents and beach huts replaced them as changing rooms – and then of course as family homes from home.

Newfoundland

We generally assume 'globalisation' is a recent phenomenon, so it may come as a surprise that when Henry VIII was on the throne Devon fishermen were regularly spending their summers in temporary camps on the shores of Newfoundland, fishing for cod on the Grand Banks, then selling the dried cod (which could keep for up to ten years) in Spain, Portugal and France.

They were by no means alone, but competed with Portuguese, Spanish and French fishermen. Trade was seriously interrupted from time to time by wars, in the seventeenth century by piracy, and on occasion by differences between the English settlers and the English fishermen, but in good times it was highly profitable. In Autumn 1595, 50 boats returned to Plymouth alone, with an estimated two million fish. In the 1620s, there may have been 10,000 men involved in the trade.

Bristolians and Devonians came to dominate the eastern seaboard of Newfoundland's Avalon peninsula, including St John's. Traditionally, fairly large vessels (of about 100 tons with perhaps 40 crew and substantial supplies) sailed on 1 March, returning at the end of September. They used smaller boats to do the fishing, mainly line fishing for medium sized cod.

So substantial were the catches that other ships, with smaller crews and plenty of space in their holds, made the journey once or twice during the summer to take the dried fish to southern European customers. These were called sac ships, possibly because they brought 'sack' back from Spain – sack being fortified white wine including sherry.

In the second half of the seventeenth century, the fishermen began to spend winters in Newfoundland, mainly to ensure that their settlements were not ransacked by others. Newfoundland remained a British colony and from 1907 an independent dominion until it joined Canada in 1949.

The Nymets

In the peaceful centre of Devon, not far from North Tawton, lie the strangely named villages of Nymet Rowland, Nymet Tracy, Nichols Nymet and Broadnymett. The origin of these names is thought to be the ancient British *nemeton*, meaning a sacred grove.

Further north are Bishop's Nympton, King's Nympton and George Nympton, but these are probably named after the River Mole, which was known at one time as the River Nymet.

The Romans built a fort at North Tawton, where their road from Exeter crossed the River Taw, and this is believed by many to have been called *Nemetostatio* – 'the fort of the sacred groves', though the identification of *Nemetostatio* is contested. If there were indeed sacred groves in the area, their exact locations are unknown.

Otters

There are once again many otters in Devon, after a period of rapid population decline largely caused by chemicals leaching into the rivers. They had been regarded as vermin, and otter hunting was only banned in 1979. The River Otter in East Devon was originally *Otrig*, probably meaning 'otter water'.

There is of course one otter more famous than any other, the eponymous hero of *Tarka the Otter* by Henry Williamson, a novel published in 1927, now regarded as a children's book but not originally conceived as such. It had taken four years of research, and is distinguished by lack of anthropomorphism: Tarka remains an otter, not some kind of cuddly human with paws and a taste for fish. Over the years the book caused a major shift in the public perception of otters, which are now a protected species.

The Pack of Cards

This bizarre house in Combe Martin, used an inn since the early 19th century, when it was known as the King's Arms, is said to have been built by George Ley with the proceeds of a win at the card table in 1690 (though some say 1626) and is an eccentric tribute to one man's luck.

With its strange construction, it resembles a house of cards, has 4 floors, 13 doors on each floor, stands apparently on a plot of land 52ft x 52ft, and (before the window tax was introduced) had 52 windows.

George Ley of Marwood was an 'overseer of the poor' and had received a licence in 1677 to run a private school in the village. George Ley's Charity, founded for educational purposes, still exists.

Pixies

The sheer unpredictability and contrariness of life, which with our superior scientific knowledge we now know to be governed by Murphy's Law, was attributed by our ancestors to the activities of Pisgy, or Puck, or Robin Goodfellow, or as the ancient Greeks knew him, the god Pan, inspirer of panic.

Before the eighteenth century most country people all over Britain probably believed in the little people. These beliefs died out slowly, and the west of England, like the Highlands of Scotland, clung hardest to them. By the time writers began to collect these tales – which till then had been told only by travelling story-tellers and by the old folk around the fireside – perhaps they were narrated with a twinkle in the eye. Yet they were often believed or part-believed by their audiences.

Some pixy stories are told in a way which suggests drunkenness, practical joking, or even crime: smugglers would spread stories of pixies, ghosts and the devil to deter people from walking at night and seeing more than they should, or to explain sudden wealth, or pack-horses mysteriously exhausted at dawn.

Yet many people really did sometimes turn their clothes inside out, or put a prayer book under their pillow, as a protective measure, and it was reported in 1879 that a Dartmoor farmer, whose cattle were dying of an infection, sacrificed a sheep to the pixies he thought were causing it, which is certainly a measure of his belief. Mothers desperate over a child with an illness or disfigurement sometimes convinced themselves that they had a changeling, rather than face up to the truth. And to be lost on a boggy moor in fog is a terrifying experience likely to make the imagination run riot. The pixies were a way of making sense of stressful events.

Today, many people believe in guardian angels, and apparently others believe that they have been abducted into alien spacecraft before being returned among us. We have no cause to think our ancestors were more credulous than us.

The Quicksilver mail coach

If you have driven down to Devon, you may have been lucky or unlucky with the traffic, but you can certainly measure your journey in hours. When the first passenger coach service started in 1658, the journey from London to Exeter took four days – better than the goods waggon which took six. Services might well be suspended in winter.

From about 1750 the roads began to be improved, and journey times improved, especially after 1820 when new turnpike roads had been built. The golden age of the mail coaches saw competition between the 'Telegraph' and the Devonport mail, popularly known as the 'Quicksilver'. The record was held by the Quicksilver, which took 16 1/2 hours from London to Exeter, and reached Devonport in 21 1/4 hours. The route taken was via Basingstoke, Salisbury, Dorchester and Honiton.

On the way the passengers were allowed just 20 minutes for breakfast and 30 minutes for dinner. At a cost of over £4 single, plus tips, it was not cheap. To protect against highwaymen, the coach had a guard with a blunderbuss, two pistols and a cutlass. Unfortunately on 20 October 1816 the guard failed to prevent an escaped lioness attacking the horses at Winterslow Hut, on the A30 five miles east of Salisbury. The menagerie owner calmed the lioness, while the passengers took refuge in the inn. He subsequently bought the injured horse, for display alongside the lioness.

Sir Walter Raleigh

John Aubrey (1626-1697), that great collector of biographical information – much of it scurrilous and too dangerous to print – made notes about Sir Walter as follows (spelling modernised):

Queen Elizabeth loved to have all the servants of her Court proper men, and Sir W.R.'s graceful presence was no mean recommendation to him. I think his first preferment at Court was Captain of Her Majesty's guard. There came a country gentleman up to town, who had several sons, but one an extraordinary proper handsome fellow, whom he did hope to have preferred to be a yeoman of the guard.

The father (a goodly man himselfe) comes to Sir Walter Raleigh, a stranger to him, and told him that he had brought up a boy that he would desire should be one of her majesty's guard. Quoth Sir Walter Raleigh, 'Had you spake for your self I should readily have granted your desire, for your person deserves it, but I put in no boys.'

Said the father, 'Boy, come in.' The son enters, about 18 or 19, but such a goodly proper young fellow as Sir Walter Raleigh had not seen the like – he was the tallest of all the guard. Sir Walter Raleigh swears him immediately; and ordered him to carry up the first dish at dinner, where the Queen beheld him with admiration, as if a beautiful young giant had stalked in with the service.

He was the first that brought tobacco into England, and into fashion. In our part of North Wiltshire, e.g. Malmesbury hundred, it came first into fashion by Sir Walter Long. I have heard my grandfather Lyte say that one pipe was handed from man to man round about the table. They had first silver pipes; the ordinary sort made use of a walnutshell and a straw.

It was sold then for its weight in silver. I have heard some of our old yeomen neighbours say that when they went to Malmesbury or Chippenham market, they culled out their biggest shillings to lay in the scales against the tobacco.

Sir W.R., standing in a stand at Sir Robert Poyntz' parke at Acton, took a pipe of tobacco, which made the ladies quit it till he had done.

Old Sir Thomas Malett, one of the justices of the King's Bench in the time of Charles I and II, knew Sir Walter; and I have heard him say that, notwithstanding his so great mastership in style and his conversation with the learnedest and politest persons, yet he spake broad Devonshire to his dying day. His voice was small, as likewise were my schoolfellows, his grandnephews.

Sir Walter Ralegh was a great chymist; and amongst some manuscript recipes, I have seen some secrets from him. He studied most in his sea-voyages, where he carried always a trunk of books along with him, and had nothing to divert him.

I have now forgotten whether Sir Walter was not for the putting of Mary, Queen of Scots, to death; I think, yea. But, besides that, at a consultation at Whitehall, after Queen Elizabeth's death, how matters were to be ordered and what ought to be done, Sir Walter Raleigh declared his opinion, 'twas the wisest way for them to keep the government in their own hands, and set up a commonwealth, and not be subject to a needy beggarly nation [i.e. they should not accept a Scottish king to rule England]. It seems there were some of this cabal who kept not this so secret but that it came to King James's ear; who, when the English noblesse met and received him, being told upon their presentment to his majesty their names, when Sir Walter Raleigh's name was told [pronounced 'Rawly'], said the king 'On my soul, mon, I have heard rawly of thee.'

Reaves

Dartmoor's reaves are one its most extraordinary features, but at first sight you might not realise why.

'Reave' is a dialect word for a hedge or wall forming a boundary division (compare the obsolete phrase 'riven in twain') and large parts of the moor are covered by these old walls, some delineating fields – 10,000 hectares of them (40 square miles) – and others separating common grazing areas belonging to different communities. The longest reave is more than 10 km in length.

Probably the best place to see them without a long walk is from Combestone Tor, west of Venford Reservoir. Look north from the parking place there, especially in evening light, and you will see on the other side of the Dart valley an extensive grid of parallel lines, meticulously laid out to create rectangular fields. If you are familiar with upland landscapes elsewhere, for example the Pennines, you will immediately think of similar grids which were laid out after Parliamentary enclosure Acts, and guess at a date around 1750.

And your date would not be far out, except that the Dartmoor reaves date not from AD 1750 but from around 1750 BC, a period know as the Late Neolithic/Early Bronze Age. If you want to see what they look like close-up, there's one running immediately on the east side of the Combestone Tor parking area – but over the millenia they were re-used in different styles, and their original structure ranged from earth banks and simple wooden fences to quite elaborate stone walls with facings and topping stones, so what matters is their straightness, not their structure.

If you were told at primary school that the Romans introduced straight lines to primitive British tribesmen, think again! These geometric grids, at precise right-angles despite very uneven ground, would be a surveying achievement now. How did Bronze

Age people achieve this degree of accuracy without modern equipment, and without maps?

The reaves also imply something about the politics and administration of the society which created them, often it seems imposing them over an earlier, more individualistic, less rigid field pattern. If it took an Act of Parliament to do this kind of thing in AD 1750, how was it done 3500 years earlier? We do not know.

Runaway Lane

This is a green lane running west from Modbury, which was the main road from Dartmouth to Plymouth as late as 1765, when Donn's map (see page 8) was published.

It gets its name from the second battle of Modbury during the English Civil War. The first battle, on 9 December 1642, was little more than a skirmish, but the second battle, on 21 February 1643, was more significant.

The King's army was besieging Plymouth, but a force of 8000 Parliamentarians collected at Kingsbridge to relieve the siege. The royalists constructed fortifications at Modbury to hold them off, and 2000 men tried to hold the position, but were unable to do so when their ammunition began to run out. They retreated along what became known as Runaway Lane. The consequence of this battle was the relief of the siege of Plymouth, and the royalist forces were pushed out of Devon into Cornwall.

Smuggling

The heyday of British smuggling was from 1700 to 1850, and Devon with its two coasts had more than its fair share of the 'free trade'. Of course there was smuggling before 1700 (when it was mainly an export industry) and it has continued ever since, but in that period it probably had the support of the majority of the population, who objected to high excise taxes imposed in order to pay for wars with France. When there were violent confrontations, it was considered impossible to get a Devon jury to convict a Devon smuggler: they were much more likely to convict the exciseman.

We tend to think of smuggling as involving mainly spirits (French brandy, Dutch gin and Caribbean rum) but thousands of other commodities were involved, including tea and silk. The south Devon trade was mostly with Guernsey until 1767 when new rules were applied. Then the French government had the clever idea of making Roscoff a free port – creating profits for themselves while depriving the British government of tax income: British merchants promptly established themselves in Roscoff. But there was also a substantial trade with incoming merchant ships on their way up the Channel or to Bristol: these ships offloaded a good part of their cargo to local smuggling vessels before reaching port.

We naturally think of the smugglers as being seamen, and many were, but the trade was financed by gentlemen and clergy, who alone had the capital, and when cargoes were landed they were brought ashore by well organised parties of agricultural labourers.

In 1783 it was estimated that 160,000 people and a fifth of the nation's horses were involved, and the annual quantity of smuggled brandy alone was six bottles for every adult in the country.

The trade was not effectively controlled until the Coast Guard Service was established in 1822, and even then corruption continued, and the smugglers became ever more ingenious – for example disguising tobacco as rope, using hollow masted vessels, 'sowing the crop' for crabbers to retrieve, and women carrying containers of alcohol beneath their skirts in order to distribute it. A fascinating description of the trade can be found in Robert Hesketh's *Devon Smugglers: the Truth behind the Fiction*.

The effective end to this period of smuggling came in the 1840s, when taxes on the smuggled items were greatly reduced, making the profit of the trade no longer worth the risks. This had been done with tea as early as 1784, but politicians never seem to learn!

Trawling

In early Victorian times Brixham's trawlers, with their red sails (weather-proofed using local red ochre), were the height of fishing technology. Although trawling had been around for centuries, the invention of beam trawling greatly increased catches. These beams, which kept the net open, were typically 48ft long (15 metres) and were slung along the port side of the boat when not in use.

So successful were they that Brixham boats first colonised the Channel ports, particularly Ramsgate, and then moved up to Hull, and later Grimsby, from which they could fish near the Dogger Bank. Soon the men began to take their families with them, and settle there rather than simply spending the summer months. An analysis of Hull fishermen in 1851 shows that more than 70% were born either in Devon, mostly Brixham, or in Kent of Devonian families, and from the birthplaces of their children it is clear that whilst some had arrived as early as 1840, the main influx was from 1847 onward. It was Devon fishermen who owned most of the trawlers in Hull, and many of the non-Devonian fishermen were their locally born apprentices.

The Devon historian WG Hoskins wrote that Hull and Grimsby 'were poor places until the Devonshire men came and showed them how to fish.' This is untrue. Kingston-upon-Hull was by no means 'a poor place' – it was England's third largest port at the time, with a huge continental trade – and the new fishing industry was regarded by many locals as an intolerable nuisance, smelly and with little boats getting in the way of the international ships.

In Grimsby it was former Thames fishermen who had settled in the early days, rather than Devonians, but those who had settled in Hull found Grimsby more attractive from 1860 onwards, and local men soon learned the techniques of the trawlers. Before long, steam trawlers were introduced, and they had great advantages over the sailing craft, because a better design of net could be used; but the Brixham men either did not have the capital to build the steamers, or were prejudiced against them, and their share of the market declined relentlessly. By 1930 Brixham's own trawler fleet had declined from 290 to just seven.

Today Brixham's fish market has revived, and is reputed to be the most important in England and Wales, if measured by the value of its trade rather than its bulk.

The Undercliff

The cliffs of south Devon are liable to crumble, and almost every year the Coast Path is subject to minor diversions. But occasionally major landslips occur, at most one or two each century, and 'undercliff' is the name given to the bizarre landscapes which result.

There are two main areas in Devon: firstly the stretch between Axmouth Harbour and Lyme Regis, where there were relatively minor events in 1828 and 1840, but a very major event in 1839. The effect was something like an earthquake. A large area of land several miles long, including some 20 hectares (50 acres) of arable land, descended 25-30 metres (80-100ft) and moved sideways, leaving a great chasm. In some cases the crops were almost undisturbed, and were subsequently harvested. A contemporary account said:

> The scene presents a spectacle not easily described – gigantic rocks having been rent asunder, lofty trees buried beneath the mighty mass, with only their tops visible; large fields with their crops, separated, one part here and another there – immense precipices formed, awful chasms which appear bottomless, the whole of which strike the beholder with terror and amazement.

Sabine Baring-Gould (see page 4) wrote a rather melodramatic novel about the events leading up to the 1839 slip, *Winefred, A Story of the Chalk Cliffs*, which is available online. And at the time of writing, the Lyme Regis Museum has put online a superb geological report from 1840, *The Bindon Landslip of 1839*, with detailed drawings, some made from a boat.

Today the Coast Path runs through the area, but it is a difficult walk, much longer than you might expect because there are so many twists and turns; one cannot leave the path, and the views are restricted. It is the nearest experience England offers to walking through a jungle!

The second area is easier of access, and is known as the Hooken Undercliff. It was formed in one night in 1790, when 4 hectares (10 acres) of land abruptly descended and moved seaward. As with the Axmouth undercliff, it has become an area of dense vegetation, with strange chalk pinnacles sticking up in front of the main cliffs. The Coast Path from Branscombe Mouth towards Beer Regis passes through it and it makes a most dramatic walk.

The VW Caravette

The Volkswagen Type 2, with the driver right at the front of the vehicle, was first produced in 1949, and before long Volkswagen were producing it as a van, a mini-bus, a flat-bed truck, an ambulance and a fire engine – and as a camper van.

In 1955 Jack White, a builder in Sidmouth, converted one for his own use, with the aid of a kitchen unit carpenter. It was so much admired by the local VW dealer that Jack White began producing conversions for sale, calling them the 'Caravette', initially in his garden shed, but then in a purpose-built factory, the Alexandria Works, on the site of the former Sidmouth gasworks.

Jack himself died of a heart attack in 1963, but before long the company were producing 1000 Caravettes a year, and in 1972, as Devon Conversions Ltd, they became the official British VW converters, selling 3500 a year. But then came the era of the package holiday. The company went into liquidation in 1985, and the name was sold: Devon Conversions now operates from County Durham.

The VW Caravette was an iconic vehicle of its time. It made travel affordable, whether for families exploring Europe, for surfers catching the waves at dawn, or for hippies seeing the world. Above all it represented freedom.

Westward Ho!

The village of Westward Ho! is the only British placename including an exclamation mark, though it is put in the shade by St Louis-du-Ha! Ha! in Quebec, which has two!!!

It is also one of the few places named after a novel – others include Waverley Station in Edinburgh, and the state of California, which appears to have been named after an imaginary island described in *Las Sergas de Esplandián*, published in 1496. [Surely that sentence deserves an exclamation mark? Ed.]

The Devon village was deliberately developed as a seaside resort by a company formed in 1863, eight years after publication of the novel. So might you want to read the novel, which is partly set in Bideford?

Westward Ho! was written during the Crimean War, a time of fanatical patriotism and gung-ho British imperialism, and celebrates the pioneering spirit of Devon's seamen of the Elizabethan era. Real people and events are mixed with invented characters and plot. Killing Spaniards is a Good Thing, especially if accompanied by swagger and swash-buckling. Even the slaughter of prisoners can be justified. It may be difficult for the reader to reconcile all this with the fact that Kingsley was a clergyman – and also that he was at one time regarded as a dangerous revolutionary.

Wine

Devon today has a number of vineyards, mostly established since 1975, but it may well be that wine-growing has a much older history. It is claimed by some modern growers that the Romans had vineyards in Devon. Whilst that is thought highly likely, since the climate was right and there are vineyards all across southern England from Dorset eastward, archaeologists tell me that there is at the time of writing no firm evidence within Devon.

The grape varieties grown in England in Roman times fared best when on chalky soil, which is largely lacking in Devon, and Devon farming was still traditional, not based on villa estates in the Roman style, either of which might explain an absence of vineyards.

Whilst there is evidence in Domesday Book that vineyards existed in 1086, or had been reintroduced into England, once again there is no evidence of them in Devon. Wine was undoubtedly imported, initially into the Roman army's supply base at Exeter from as early as AD 55 and then later for the civilian population.

And in the Middle Ages the port of Dartmouth became rich by importing wine, and exporting woollen cloth. In 1408 the English 'wine fleet' consisted of 200 ships, and of those no fewer than 27 came from Dartmouth. At that time Bordeaux was a possession of the English crown, but it was finally lost in 1451 – and Dartmouth stagnated for the next hundred years or more. From Elizabethan times Devon seamen took Newfoundland cod to Italy, Spain and Portugal, and purchased wine there for importing into England.

Today's Devon vineyards produce a wide variety of wine types, Champagne-style sparkling wines and Pinot Noir red, as well as the white and rosé varieties you might expect. Many of the vineyards are open to the public, and some have cafés. The Visit Devon site on the internet has all the details.

The witches of Bideford

Every county in England had its historic witch trials, but Devon was perhaps the last place where 'witches' were actually hanged.

Temperance Lloyd, aged 80, Mary Trembles and Susanna Edwards were all found guilty by magistrates at Bideford in 1682. They were blamed for causing illnesses but the evidence against them was to modern thinking absurd – accounts of a magpie and a cat being seen to enter a bedroom, marks on victims' bodies that could only have been caused by a witch driving pins into a stolen doll, and a range of hearsay 'confessions' – but in court all three actually admitted their guilt, and described the devil as a miniature black man with saucer eyes, whom they allowed to suck at their breasts.

An instruction sheet issued to magistrates nearly a century earlier gave 40 characteristics by which to identify witches, for example:

> They are most comonly weeke women.
> They are such as are of malicious dispositions.
> They are most comonly poor and very myserable.
> They wil be in desolate places, looking of strange hearbs…

So it's hardly surprising that

> They thinke everie thinge prouffes against them.
> They will therfor deny trewthes not materiall.

Even herbal medicine was a suspicious activity, and being poor and begging for food, as the three Bideford witches were, was almost enough in itself.

They were sent to Exeter for trial at the assizes, where public interest was soon at fever pitch. In most witch trials by 1682 the judges acquitted the accused, but at this trial, where the accused had proclaimed their own guilt, Lord North was convinced that a not-guilty verdict would suggest the law no longer believed in witchcraft, leading to a popular uprising, inevitably followed by illegal witch-hunts. So all three were found guilty, and hanged at Heavitree on 25 August 1682.

Why did they 'confess'? Probably they believed they had special powers: that delusion would perhaps be a comfort to women who were actually powerless, and rejected by their own communities.

At a later trial in Exeter in 1685, one Alice Molland was accused of witchcraft and condemned to death, but it is uncertain whether she was hanged.

Exe

(Sorry, best I could think of – and the great traveller Celia Fiennes did call the river the X!) The Exe is one of 11 rivers in Britain – Axe, Esk, Usk etc – which take their name from the old British word *isca*, which meant water, or specifically river. The same word gives us usquebaugh, the water of life, better known as whisky.

The Devon Exe actually rises in Somerset, near Simonsbath on Exmoor, and of course it gives its name to numerous settlements from Exford to Exmouth. The most significant feature of the river is its broad estuary, with the tidal limit fixed at Countess Wear, a weir having been built under the orders of Isabella de Fortibus, Countess of Devon, probably in 1284.

Topsham, below the weir, may well have been the port of Exeter in Roman times, but was certainly so in late medieval times – much to the benefit of the Earls of Devon, who were able to impose heavy tolls on goods going to and from the city. The Exeter Canal was completed in 1566 and greatly improved in 1701 to enable ships to reach Exeter Quay.

Yorkshire fish and chips

What, you might ask, has this to do with Devon? A lot, actually! See the article on Trawling on page 33. Railways had reached Hull in 1840 and Grimsby in 1844. At more or less the same time, Brixham fishermen, with their superior trawling equipment, began to exploit new fishing grounds in the North Sea.

They landed large quantities of fish at both Hull and Grimsby, and this found a ready market among the working classes in the industrial towns of the West Riding, where many women were employed full time, and had no time to cook for their families, even if they had cooking facilities in their houses – which many did not.

Fish and chips caught on as the obvious ready meal. So Brixham was responsible for Yorkshire's unhealthy diet, though it can plead not guilty to the lesser charge: it has no responsibility for mushy peas.

Zeal Monachorum

This was said by the historian WG Hoskins in 1954 to be 'a small village of cob and thatch in unfrequented country', which remains a reasonable description.

Its intriguing name is an enthusiastic adaptation of the Latin *cella monachorum*. Whilst *monachorum* indisputably means 'of the monks' there is little agreement about which of the many meanings of *cella* we should choose.

In medieval Latin it often meant 'daughter house', but although Buckfast Abbey (the original Benedictine abbey founded in 1018) was said to have been given the manor of Zeal by King Cnut, and certainly owned it at the time of the Domesday survey, there is no evidence of a daughter house. Perhaps *cella* was used in one of its original classical Latin meanings, as a storehouse or granary.

Zzzzz.